WEATHER
PATTERNS

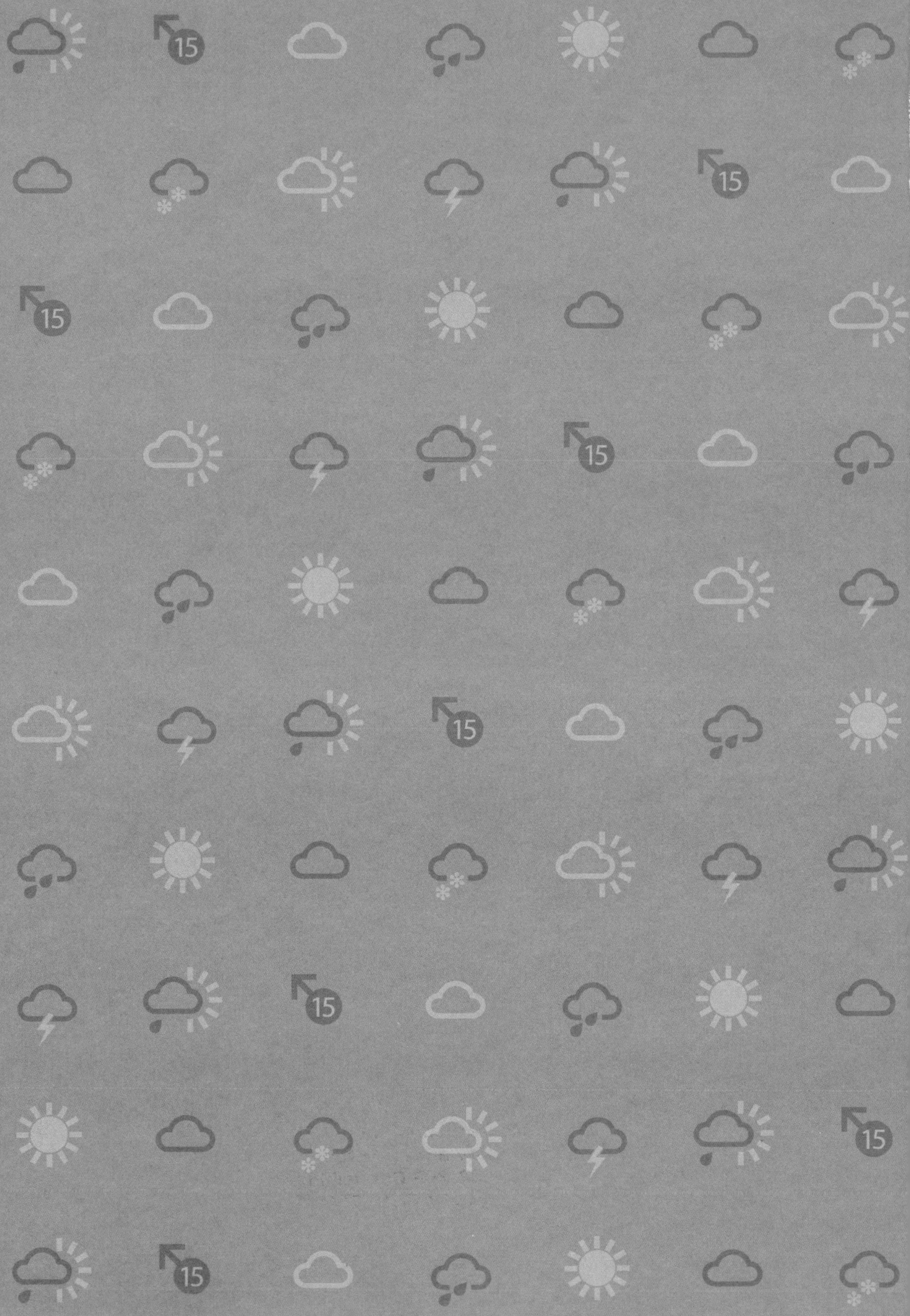

WEATHER AND CLIMATE

WEATHER PATTERNS

Terry Jennings

Evans

First published 2005 by Evans Brothers Limited
2A Portman Mansions
Chiltern Street
London W1U 6NR

British Library Cataloguing in Publication Data

Jennings, Terry J.
Weather pattern. - (Weather and climate)
1.Weather - Juvenile literature 2.Weather forecasting -
Juvenile literature 3.Climatology - Juvenile literature
I.Title
551.6

ISBN 0237527472

Designer: Giraffic Design
Editor: Mary-Jane Wilkins
Illustrator: Graham Rosewarne
Series consultant: Steve Watts

Picture acknowledgements
Ecoscene: page 7 (top and bottom), 17 (bottom), 27 (bottom),
31 (bottom), 35 (top), 38, 40
Terry Jennings: page 2, 5, 14, 25 (middle), 26 (top and bottom),
27 (top), 29, 31 (middle), 34, 36, 37 (top and bottom), 44,
45 (bottom)
Oxford Scientific: page 6, 10, 15 (bottom), 28, 45 (top)
Still Pictures: front cover, page 15 (middle), 17 (top), 18,
19 (top and bottom), 20, 21 (top and bottom), 22 (middle and
bottom), 23, 24, 25 (top), 30, 31 (top), 32, 33 (top and bottom),
35 (bottom), 37 (middle), 39 (top and bottom), 41, 42 (top and
bottom), 43

Contents

Changing weather

The weather changes from hour to hour and day to day. The Sun may shine for a short time, then dark clouds quickly cover the sky. The temperature falls and it may pour with rain before the skies clear and the Sun comes out again.

If we look at the weather over many years, we can see a pattern. In the British Isles, northern Europe, central North America and other places in the middle latitudes, summers are warm while winters are cold with ice and snow. Rainfall in June is about the same as in November. A typical pattern of weather over many years makes up the climate of a region.

The Painted Desert in north-east Arizona in the United States. Deserts have less than 250mm of rain a year on average. Some years they have no rain at all.

Climate variation

Climates vary enormously around the world. They affect the character of an area, the plants and animals that live there, the people and the homes they live in. Near the Equator the climate is hot and mostly wet. Deserts are dry, while the poles have year-round ice and snow.

There are also smaller climates, called microclimates. Cities are often warmer than the countryside. Valley bottoms may be protected from strong winds, but they are in the cold shadow of the hills around them. Different world climates result partly from the Sun, which shines more strongly at the tropics than elsewhere, and partly from the way in

The polar bear is superbly adapted to life in the Arctic. Its white coat acts as camouflage, while its dense fur and thick layer of fat protect it from the extreme cold.

which the Earth's atmosphere and oceans transfer heat away from the Equator to other parts of the Earth's surface. If the Earth had no atmosphere or oceans, it would have no climates.

Both weather and climate have the same elements: temperature, rainfall, wind, air pressure, humidity, cloud, sunshine and so on. The two most important are mean (average) temperatures and mean rainfall. The Sun supplies the energy to power our weather. It also produces the energy to make water evaporate from the oceans and seas. But to reach the Earth, the Sun's rays have to pass through the atmosphere.

The atmosphere

The atmosphere forms several layers around the Earth. The lowest is the troposphere. It rises above the Earth for about 16 km over the Equator and about 8 km above the poles. This is the layer in which all life exists, and where all our weather occurs.

The air consists of three gases: nitrogen, oxygen and argon in constant proportions. It also has variable amounts of water vapour, and tiny quantities of several gases, including carbon dioxide, neon, helium, krypton, xenon, methane and ozone. These other gases make up 0.04 per cent of the atmosphere by volume. Also in the air are dust, smoke and salt particles and pollen grains.

Air pressure

When we walk on the Earth's surface we are in effect walking at the bottom of a sea of air. Air seems to weigh nothing, but in fact it has substance and is many kilometres deep. The average classroom probably contains more than 100 kg of air, and air presses down on every square centimetre of the Earth with a force of about 1 kg. This means that there is a force of about 1 kg pressing down on one of your fingernails. But air presses in all directions, not just downwards, which is why we are not squashed flat by it.

This smoke pollution is coming from a power station in an industrial area of northern China.

THE EFFECT OF THE CURVATURE OF THE EARTH ON THE SUN'S RAYS

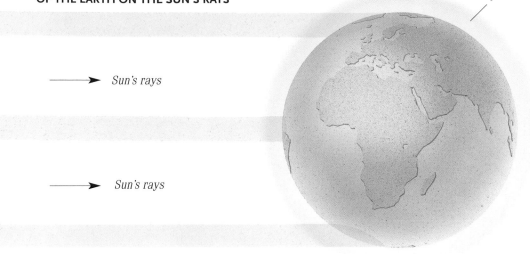

atmosphere

Sun's rays

Sun's rays

Air pressure and wind

Air pressure varies from time to time and place to place. When the air pressure is different in two places near each other, it creates wind. Wind is moving air that blows from an area of high pressure to an area of low pressure until the two pressures have equalised. Variations in air pressure are caused by differences in the warming power of the Sun.

The Earth is a sphere, so the Sun heats the tropics more than the poles. The Sun's rays hit the area around the Equator full on and make this the hot region of the Earth. Near the poles the Sun's rays strike the Earth at a low angle. They spread over a wider area, and warm it less.

The climate of a place depends on how far it is from the Equator. This distance, latitude, is measured in degrees. But three other factors also affect climate. The equatorial regions are often covered with cloud which moderates the temperature. Second, large blocks of land heat up and cool down faster than the surrounding ocean. Third, temperature drops with altitude, so the highest mountains are covered with ice and snow throughout the year.

Seasonal changes

Weather changes regularly through the year. Places between the Equator and the poles, the middle latitudes, have four seasons. We have seasons because the Earth is tilted on its axis and it remains tilted at the same angle as it circles the Sun. So, for part of the year the northern hemisphere is tilted towards the Sun, giving that part of the world the long, warm days of summer. At the same time, the southern hemisphere, tilted away from the Sun, has the shorter, cooler days of winter. When the Earth travels to the far side of the Sun, the southern hemisphere is tilted towards the Sun and the seasons reverse.

COLDEST PLACE

The world's coldest place is Plateau Station in Antarctica. The average annual temperature is -57°C. The world's lowest temperature of -88°C was recorded during a storm at the Vostok Scientific Station in Antarctica, about 150 km from the South Pole.

Towards the Equator, places are less affected by the Earth's tilt and the climate is more constant. Although the seasons are not hot and cold in these places, they are often divided into a rainy season and a dry season. At the poles there are only summer and winter seasons.

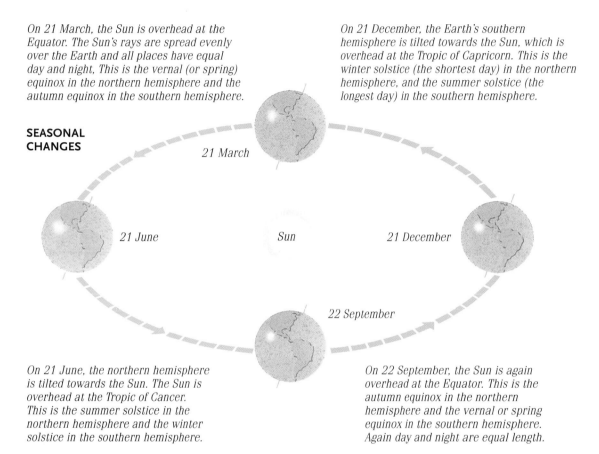

On 21 March, the Sun is overhead at the Equator. The Sun's rays are spread evenly over the Earth and all places have equal day and night, This is the vernal (or spring) equinox in the northern hemisphere and the autumn equinox in the southern hemisphere.

On 21 December, the Earth's southern hemisphere is tilted towards the Sun, which is overhead at the Tropic of Capricorn. This is the winter solstice (the shortest day) in the northern hemisphere, and the summer solstice (the longest day) in the southern hemisphere.

SEASONAL CHANGES

21 March

21 June

Sun

21 December

22 September

On 21 June, the northern hemisphere is tilted towards the Sun. The Sun is overhead at the Tropic of Cancer. This is the summer solstice in the northern hemisphere and the winter solstice in the southern hemisphere.

On 22 September, the Sun is again overhead at the Equator. This is the autumn equinox in the northern hemisphere and the vernal or spring equinox in the southern hemisphere. Again day and night are equal length.

The effect of relief

The relief, or shape, of the landscape also affects the climate. Warm, moist winds, forced to rise by a mountain range, lose most of their moisture as rain or snow on the windward side of the mountains. But when the winds blow down the sheltered, or leeward, side of the mountain they become warmer as they descend and evaporate moisture from the land. Areas on the leeward side of mountains are often very dry, or even desert. They are said to be in a rain shadow. Many of the world's great deserts were formed as a result of this rain shadow effect.

The climate of mountain regions is colder than the surrounding lowland areas, because the Sun does not warm the air directly. It heats the Earth, which warms the air above it so the higher you go above the Earth, the less the air is warmed. On average the temperature falls 2°C for every 300m you climb. This affects the wild plants or crops that can grow on a mountain and explains why the tops of many high mountains, even near the Equator, are covered in snow for all or most of the year.

Sea fog surrounds a fishing boat off the coast of Maine in the US. It forms when warm air over a warm ocean current drifts over a cold current and condensation occurs.

Land and sea

Places near the sea have a milder and wetter climate (called a maritime climate) than places further inland. This is because sea water can hold a lot more heat than land. When the Sun's heat strikes the land, only a thin layer of soil and rock absorbs the heat. Over the oceans and seas the heat penetrates deeply and warms up a much greater volume. It takes a lot of heat energy to warm up an ocean, but once it is warm it takes a long time to cool down. By contrast, the land warms up quickly but also loses its heat quickly. So the temperatures of places near the sea are not as extreme as those far inland. The climates of inland areas are called continental climates.

The differences between a maritime and a continental climate are shown by the temperatures of Edinburgh and Moscow, both similar distances north of the Equator. The mean maximum temperature in Edinburgh in January is 6°C and in July 18°C. By contrast the mean maximum temperature in Moscow is -9°C in January and 23°C in July. Moscow has extreme temperatures because it is far inland, whereas Edinburgh, close to the sea, has a more moderate climate.

Ocean currents

Sea water is always moving – in waves, tides and currents. Warm water from the tropics flows towards the poles, while cold water from the polar regions flows towards the Equator. Sometimes these currents form a definite stream, such as the Gulf Stream. Most currents are caused by winds that blow in the same direction all the time, although some are caused by differences in salinity. Currents can be altered by the Coriolis effect, the spinning of the Earth, and by coastlines. The result is a complicated pattern of ocean currents across the world.

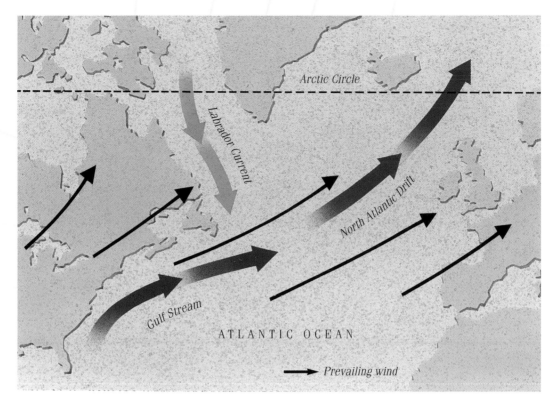

This map shows the main ocean currents in the North Atlantic. The black arrows show the direction of the prevailing winds.

The Gulf Stream is one of the most important ocean currents. It begins with warm (26-29°C) water near the Equator in the Gulf of Mexico. This warm current flows up the east coast of the United States, warming the land. The Gulf Stream then flows across the Atlantic Ocean and fans out as the North Atlantic Drift. The warm air over the Gulf Stream and the North Atlantic Drift brings milder winters to parts of north-west Europe than you would expect for places so far north of the Equator. Without it, the sea around Scandinavia and northern Britain would freeze in winter. Cold currents have the opposite effect.

Warm winds

Winds blowing over warm ocean currents to the land are also warmed. Because these winds have a higher temperature they are moist and often bring rain. Winds blowing over cold currents, such as the Labrador Current, do not hold much moisture and so dry the land.

The effect of an ocean on the temperature becomes less the further away from it you go. The British Isles receive their prevailing winds from the south-west. These winds were formed over the Atlantic Ocean and warmed by the Gulf Stream and North Atlantic Drift. They are relatively warm in winter and cool in summer, and produce similar temperatures over the British Isles. The eastern coast of the United States also receives its prevailing winds from the south-west, but these winds originate over the North American continent. As a result, the eastern coast of the United States has hot summers, cold winters and a great annual range of temperature.

EXTREME TEMPERATURES

At Tromso in Norway, north of the Arctic Circle, the lowest temperature recorded is -18°C. In the Karakum Desert in Turkmenistan, 3,000 km further south, the lowest temperature is -32°C.

Climatic regions

The average weather conditions of a place are called its climate. The most important conditions are the mean (average) monthly temperatures and the mean monthly rainfall. Scientists divide the world into regions according to their climate, although the boundaries are not sharply defined, as one type of climate merges gradually into the next.

- Polar (Arctic/Antarctic)
- Arctic tundra
- Mountains
- Coniferous forests
- Temperate forests
- Grasslands and savanna
- Scrublands
- Deserts
- Tropical forests

The first person to divide the world into climatic zones was the Greek philosopher Aristotle (384-322 BC). He divided the world into three zones based on the height of the Sun above the horizon.

Aristotle's three zones were the torrid, temperate and frigid zones. Modern climatic maps show many more regions, based only partly on latitude. Height above sea level and distance from the ocean are just as important. Some of the names of these climate types refer to the typical vegetation that adapted to living in that particular climate.

There are six main climatic regions, which can be further subdivided. Each zone has its own wildlife, particularly trees.

The world's desert regions have a mean yearly rainfall of less than 250 mm. The true hot deserts have high daytime temperatures. Although temperatures may drop sharply at night, there is no real cool season. The cold desert areas at higher latitudes have huge extremes of temperatures, with warm to hot summers and cold to very cold winters.

Mountain regions contain various climatic zones according to the altitude or height. This is partly because temperature drops with increasing height, but also because mountain climates are wetter than the nearby lowlands. As a result, mountain vegetation changes with height, and above the tree-line there is often permanent snow.

Polar regions are very cold with a mean temperature of less than 10°C in the warmest month. The winters are long. Most of the Arctic is covered by the Arctic Ocean which is fed with water from further south. Antarctica is colder because it is a continent and is also high above sea level. The low temperatures mean that the air can hold very little moisture. In the vast flat tundra regions around the Arctic, and near the summits of high mountains, it is too cold for trees to grow.

The cold temperate regions of the northern hemisphere are warmer than the polar regions and the mean temperature in the warmest month is over 10°C. Oceanic climates have a relatively small temperature range, whereas continental climates have a warm to hot summer and a very cold winter, with some rain in all seasons. The cold snowy regions contain huge coniferous forests.

The warm temperate regions have mean temperatures of not more than 18°C in the warmest month. There is a definite cool season and the mean temperature in the coldest month is more than -3°C.

Arctic Circle

Tropic of Cancer

Equator

Tropic of Capricorn

Tropical rainy regions have mean monthly temperatures of more than 18°C throughout the year. In tropical rainforest areas there is no real dry season and it rains all year round. The tropical monsoon areas have distinct dry and wet seasons.

Antarctic Circle

Climate and life

All known life exists naturally within a very narrow belt close to the surface of the Earth. People and other living things have been sent into space for research purposes, but these are exceptions to the general rule.

Soil, water and plant life

The Earth consists of large land masses and even larger oceans. Much of the land is covered with a thin layer of soil that teems with insect and other animal life. From this soil, thousands of different species of plants obtain the support, the mineral salts and water they need to survive. Other plants are adapted to life in the sea and freshwater environments. The distribution of plants over the world as a whole depends largely on the climate. Large ecosystems that have similar vegetation, animals and climates are called biomes. The amount of light, wind and rainfall, type of soil, and temperature all help to determine which plants and animals live there. Scientists cannot all agree on the number of biomes on land, but the six most widely accepted ones are: tropical rainforest, desert, deciduous forest, grassland, tundra and taiga. Taiga is a Russian word used for the great coniferous forests of the northern hemisphere.

Plant adaptations

In the warmer parts of the Arctic lands, ice and snow melt in summer and mosses, lichens, grasses and small flowering plants grow thinly on the stony ground. This area is known as the tundra. It is too cold for trees to grow. Most coniferous trees are adapted to cold temperate climates with warm summers. In the middle latitudes there are several vegetation zones, including grasslands, deciduous (broad-leaved) forests and Mediterranean lands. Few plants grow in the hottest deserts, but xerophytes (plants adapted to dry conditions) are able

The mountain avens grows in the Arctic tundra and on high mountain pastures. There it survives extreme cold, strong winds, a short growing season and burial under deep snow.

MUSK OX

The musk ox of Northern Canada and Greenland has hair 60 90 cm long. It can live in temperatures as low as -27°C. Without its thick, warm coat it would quickly freeze to death.

to survive in desert and semi-desert areas. The few trees able to grow in the desert have very long roots to reach the water far below the surface. The roots of some African and Australian acacia trees penetrate over 15m. Creosote and mesquite bushes have similar long taproots. Other plants that can resist drought may have large numbers of shallow roots, which collect water after every downpour. Cacti and euphorbias, another group of desert plants, store water in their fleshy stems. These swell when there is plenty of water, and shrink in times of drought. The leaves of cacti are reduced to spines which lessens the evaporation of water, and protects the plants from animals.

A mangrove swamp in an estuary in Panama. Mangroves have thick, succulent leaves with a waxy coating which protects them from salt. They excrete the salt they take up from the water through their leaves.

Mangrove trees

Mangrove trees live in the thick mud where tropical rainforests meet the sea. They live in black mud, starved of oxygen and with their roots covered in salt water – conditions which would kill most plants. As there is no oxygen in the mud, the tree roots poke out into the air, from which they absorb oxygen directly. Mangrove swamps are home to many amazing animals, including mudskipper fish that walk on land and crab-eating frogs. Mangrove roots reduce the power of the waves, and fish, crabs and prawns breed in the water round them.

Gerbils – desert animals

There are 70 species of gerbils, which live in desert and semi-desert environments. They are all adapted to habitats where water is scarce. They have amazingly efficient kidneys, which produce urine several times more concentrated than that of other rodents, conserving water. To keep their bodies as far as possible from the burning sand, gerbils have long hind legs and feet, with soles insulated with dense pads of fur. Their bellies are pure white to reflect the heat radiated from the ground. Gerbils also adapt to desert life by coming out only at night when the air is cooler. They are seed-eaters and make stores of food during the brief periods when desert plants flower and produce seeds.

A hairy-footed gerbil in the Namib Desert in south-west Africa. Gerbils are well adapted to a habitat where water is scarce.

The tropics

The tropics lie between the Tropic of Cancer and the Tropic of Capricorn. Only in this zone is the Sun ever directly overhead. It includes parts of North and South America, Africa, South and South-East Asia and Australia. In the tropics temperatures are always high, except in highland areas, and the seasons are marked only by changes in wind and rainfall.

Tropical rainforests

In moist tropical areas it rains nearly every day and it is hot throughout the year. Large areas are covered with thick, lush forests, called tropical rainforests.

Inside the rainforests it is damp and dark. As the trees grow, they compete to reach the light, spreading their branches. Some trees stretch up 60m and are close enough for their crowns to overlap.

Beneath this layer are others made by smaller trees, and masses of creepers and rope-like lianas hanging from the trunks and branches, trying to reach the light. Other plants, such as bromeliads and some orchids, grow on the upper branches of the trees. The trees support them and enable them to reach the light, but the plants make their own food. The trees shade the forest floor and there is little light, so rainforests have very little undergrowth.

Rainforest areas

The two largest areas of tropical rainforest are in the Amazon River basin in South America and in the Zaire (or Congo) basin in Africa. The Amazon River basin has a mean yearly rainfall of 2,000 mm. The Amazon forest is so large that it creates its own climate and half the rainfall comes from water vapour that has evaporated from the trees. The African forests receive less rain, but vast areas have more than 1,300 mm a year.

Super-canopy

Canopy

Understorey

Forest floor

Tropical rainforests occupy only about 7 per cent of the world's land area, but contain about 50 per cent of the world's plant and animal species.

Daily climates

In the tropics the high Sun beams a lot of energy on to the surface of the Earth and the lower layers of the atmosphere. The weather is the same almost every day. The Sun rises at about 6am and the early morning mists disperse. As the Sun rises higher in the sky the temperature goes up, and a lot of water evaporates from the rivers and forests. The air rises and cools and water vapour condenses to form great masses of clouds. During the afternoon there is a torrential downpour. The clouds then break up, and at about 6pm the Sun sets and night begins. The weather is always humid and sticky, as well as hot, and there are no summer and winter seasons.

Animal life

The layered structure of the forest gives different amounts of light and heat from top to bottom. Thousands of plants inhabit the rainforest and they support multitudes of animals. Around a million different species of plant and animal live in the Amazon rainforest. Scientists estimate that there are 1,600 different species of bird in the Amazon alone, and 40,000 different kinds of insect in just one hectare of the rainforest.

Trees and soils

Most trees are evergreens. With little change in the climate through the year, there is no particular season for the trees to flower and fruit. Individual trees lose their leaves gradually and the forest floor is covered by a thick, spongy layer of decaying leaves which break down quickly. The roots of the fast-growing trees and other plants quickly take up the mineral salts they need to grow. Such rich plant growth suggests that the soil is fertile, but the soil itself does not contain many mineral salts; they are in the vegetation. When the tree cover is removed, the heavy rainfall soon washes the plant foods out of the thin reddish soils and the soil may be eroded away.

Many of the bird species of the rainforest, such as this blue and gold macaw, are brightly coloured.

People of the rainforests

The native peoples of the rainforest have lived there for about 20,000 years. Many Amerindians in the Amazon basin and the pygmies of Africa live off the land. Everything they need for survival is there – building materials, food, transport, medicines, clothing and decoration. All the different native rainforest people are experts at surviving in this hostile environment, as well as in caring for and respecting it.

LUNGS OF THE EARTH

One third of all the world's oxygen, needed by every living thing on Earth, is produced by the tropical rainforests.

A Yanomami family in their home in the tropical rainforest of Venezuela, South America. The Yanomami are threatened by forest clearance.

Farming in the rainforest

Most farmers live at a subsistence level, growing only enough food crops, such as cassava and manioc, to feed their families. They often practise shifting cultivation, clearing a plot to farm it for a few years until the heavy rain has washed the minerals from the soil, making it infertile. They then move on to a new plot. There are also large plantations that produce cocoa, coffee, palm oil, rubber and sugar cane. Many of these are exported.

Travel and settlements

Travelling through the rainforests is difficult. Most villages and towns are on the riverbanks and, because of the risk of flooding, the houses are often built on stilts. The rivers are the main routes for local people who carry forest products in dugout canoes and other boats. Larger boats take out the heavier forest products.

EXTINCTION

Scientists estimate that between 5 and 15 per cent of rainforest species could be extinct within the next 30 years – before many of them have even been identified.

Logging and wood for fuel

About a third of the Earth's original forests have been cut down. In some parts of the world, including Europe and Asia, this deforestation started long ago. But the clearance of the rainforests, where the wildlife is richest, started on a large scale only about 50 years ago. Today, tropical rainforests are disappearing at a record rate. Many valuable tree species are scattered through the forests, including mahogany, teak and rosewood. Cutting down trees for industrial timber is one of the largest causes of deforestation. Much of the hardwood is exported to developed countries, where it ends up as

Using fire to clear the Amazon rainforest in Brazil. A forest area the size of France has been cleared for farmland in Brazil alone.

doors and window frames, lavatory seats, furniture and flooring. The loggers take only one tree in 20 in the forest, but their machinery damages 60 per cent of the other trees. Another major cause of deforestation is the cutting down of trees to provide fuel for the growing number of people living in the rainforest areas.

Farmland and beefburgers

Much of the beef for America's beefburgers is imported from Brazil. Large areas of rainforest have been cut down to make way for cattle ranches. The grazing land is cheap, so the beef is cheap. This trade in beef is vital to the economy of the countries exporting it. The heavy rain soon washes the mineral salts out of the soil, making the grassland infertile so more forest is cleared to provide grazing. Poor farmers often clear trees to grow food for themselves and their families.

Roads, plantations and mining

During the past few years, more than 10,000 km of roads have been driven through the Amazon rainforest. Some faster-growing foreign trees are grown for wood pulp to make paper and rayon. Large areas are also cleared in the search for minerals. This industry often pollutes the rivers that flow through the forest.

Constructing a road through the Amazon rainforest with heavy machinery.

Clearing the rainforest deprives the native tribes of their homes and way of life. As well as endangering many wild plants and animals, it deprives the world of many possible future foods, drugs and medicines. About a quarter of the drugs and medicines that doctors use today were developed from rainforest plants and animals. Scientists estimate that about 1,600 rainforest plants could be used as vegetables. Forest clearance is also speeding up global warming.

Monsoon climates

Some areas of the tropics have a period of torrential rain caused by seasonal winds, known as the monsoon. The word comes from the Arabic term meaning season. Arabs use this word for winds that blow for half the year from the south-west and half the year from the south-east.

Monsoon seasons

Many tropical areas experience monsoons, including the south-western United States and Chile. The strongest monsoons occur in southern Asia, northern Australia and off the coast of West Africa. Southern Asia has the most dramatic. In winter the Asian land mass cools quickly. The cold, dense air forms a large area of high pressure from which dry north-east trade winds blow. They cross the Equator and bring a hot, wet monsoon to the coastal regions of northern Australia.

Between March and May, the overhead Sun moves north, heating the land. Warm air rises, creating a large low pressure area. In June,

People wade through floodwater in Dhaka, the capital of Bangladesh, after heavy monsoon rains in September 1998.

RAINIEST PLACE

The world's rainiest place is Mawsynram, in north-east India. During the monsoon season, rainfall varies between light and heavy, but totals about 12m a year. This is one of the few places on Earth where rainfall is measured in metres rather than in millimetres.

south-east trade winds are sucked across the Equator and the Indian Ocean into this low pressure area. These warm, moist monsoon winds bring torrential rain to coastal and upland areas.

Before a monsoon, the air is stiflingly hot and very humid. Then the monsoon breaks and it may rain for weeks. Monsoon winds blow in India from June to mid-December, but some years they arrive weeks late; and occasionally fail to appear at all. There may be such heavy rain that rivers overflow, people and livestock drown and crops are destroyed. But if the rains fail, droughts cause starvation. A number of serious diseases spread after the monsoon season, including typhoid and cholera, while stagnant water becomes a breeding ground for the mosquitoes that carry malaria, yellow fever and other diseases.

Farming in monsoon areas

About a quarter of the world's people live in monsoon areas. These include some of the world's most densely-populated regions. Many people grow their own food and farm even the most steeply sloping land. To prevent the soil being washed away, farmers build a series of level, step-like terraces down the slopes.

The main crops are rice and tea, which grow well in wet conditions. When the rains arrive, the fields are flooded. Workers transplant young rice plants into the flooded fields. The plants grow in water until they start to ripen, when the fields are drained for the harvest.

Rice is an important food crop for many developing nations because it can be grown cheaply and in large quantities. The world's leading rice producers are China, India, Indonesia and Bangladesh. Farmers also grow cotton, tea and jute for export.

Monsoon forests

Monsoon forests are less dense than tropical rainforests, with shorter trees and fewer species. Many shed their leaves in the dry season, to reduce water loss. They channel their energy into flower and fruit production. Some animals living here, such as lizards, cats and monkeys, migrate along the river banks at the beginning of the dry season, to where the trees remain in leaf. Some animals change their diet, and some rodents bury nuts and seeds for when food is scarce. Birds such as toucans and macaws, which feed on fruit and nuts, nest and produce eggs and young during the dry season when the trees bear their fruits and seeds.

Rice being planted in flooded paddy fields in Java, Indonesia.

Terraced farmland on the island of Bali, Indonesia.

Tropical grasslands

Tropical or savanna grasslands are flat open plains in the central parts of the continents. They lie between 50° and 150° north and south of the Equator. Here it is hot all the year round and there is 250-750 mm of rain a year – too little for a forest and too much for a desert.

Semi-arid regions with large expanses of grassland have two seasons a year. In the wet season the grasses grow tall and green and in the dry season the vegetation is brown and parched. Most trees cannot grow under these conditions. The few that do have long roots to draw water from deep underground.

Savannas of the world

There are savanna grasslands in South America, Africa and northern Australia. During the wet season trees bear leaves and flowers. In the dry season they lose their leaves while the grasses turn brown and do not grow again until the rains return.

This leopard is a typical carnivore of the African savanna grasslands.

Fire often sweeps across the savanna in the dry season. It may burn the trees and shrubs, although the trunks of acacia trees resist fire.

The African savannas

The savannas of Africa are home to big game animals. Huge herds of antelopes, buffaloes and zebras roam the grassy plains. Elephants, rhinoceroses and giraffes feed among the thorny bushes. These herbivores may migrate long distances in the dry season to where grasses are still growing. They provide food for carnivores such as lions, cheetahs, leopards, hyenas and hunting dogs.

Large areas of the African savannas are set aside as national parks and game reserves.

The tropical grasslands that cover much of East Africa are famous for their wildlife. This buffalo has two oxpeckers on its back.

LARGEST RANCH

The world's largest cattle ranch is in Australia. It has an area of 30,000 km² – about three-quarters the size of the Netherlands.

Tourists visit and hunting is not allowed, although illegal hunting, or poaching, can be a problem.

Among the people who live in the African savannas are the Maasai, herdsmen who live on the borders of Kenya and Tanzania. They move with their herds across the grassland. When all the grass in one area has been eaten, they move to a new area. Other savanna tribes practise shifting cultivation, clearing a small area with fire. In the rainy season, they plant crops, which are fertilized by the ashes. After a few years the plant foods in the soil have been used up or washed away. The people then move on. Where there is enough water there are large modern farms growing sugar cane, maize, coffee, groundnuts, cotton, tobacco and pineapples.

The Australian savanna

Much of northern Australia is savanna grassland. Wild animals here include large numbers of plant-eating kangaroos, wallabies and emus, while dingoes are the main carnivores. The grassland is mainly used for rearing cattle. It takes more than 20 hectares of land to feed each animal. The cattle farms are called cattle stations and each covers several thousand square kilometres.

The Brazilian campo

Brazil in South America has a type of savanna grassland called campo. It lies south of the Amazon rainforests and covers an area of about 2,400 by 2,750 km. Just beneath the soil is a hard crust of iron oxides. Grasses can grow in the shallow soil, but in most places tree roots cannot penetrate the hard layer to reach the water below. There are few wild animals – grass-eating rodents, deer and two species of rhea.

THE SERENGETI

The Serengeti Plain is a vast area of savanna grassland in East Africa. Every June, the dry season forces the world's most spectacular migration. About a million wildebeest, zebras and gazelles move from the western Serengeti to the northern rivers. When the rains return, the animals move to the south-east to breed, before heading west to begin the cycle again.

A Maasai herdsman with his cattle. The Maasai people live on the borders of Kenya and Tanzania.

Deserts

Hot deserts and semi-desert regions occupy one fifth of the world's land surface. Deserts are dry, barren places, with less than 250 mm of rain each year. Where there is water, deserts are extremely rich and fertile. Some of the world's earliest civilizations grew up along the banks of rivers in desert areas.

DEATH VALLEY

Death Valley in California is the driest, hottest place in North America. It was named after gold prospectors died there in 1849, when they ran out of food and water.

Where are the deserts?

Most deserts lie near the tropics north and south of the Equator. Death Valley in California and parts of the Sahara Desert are the hottest places on Earth during daytime. But at night they become cool. During the day the Sun is intensely hot because there are few clouds. Temperatures can be over 50°C. At night, the lack of clouds allows heat to escape and temperatures may drop below freezing. Further from the Equator, the Gobi Desert in Mongolia can be extremely cold, -40°C in winter, even though it can be 45 or 50°C in summer.

Desert rain and flooding

Less than 250 mm of rain falls on a desert each year, often in short, violent storms. Rainwater can flood the hard, sun-baked ground. Flash floods happen when water rushes down gullies and valleys carrying everything before it. It carves out deep canyons. After a flood the desert rivers and streams dry up as the water soaks into the ground.

The most famous geographical features of the Sahara Desert are its large ergs, or sand seas. Some dunes are 300m high.

Desert landscapes

There are three main types of desert: sandy deserts or ergs, rocky deserts or hammada and stony deserts or reg. Deserts are made in different ways, but they are always formed because there is not enough water. Only about 25 per cent of the world's deserts are sandy.

How deserts are formed

The two bands of deserts in the hottest part of the world, north and south of the Equator, are called tropical deserts. Clouds carrying rain don't reach the Sahara and Kalahari deserts. Places in the middle of continents, such as Central Asia, are deserts because they are too far from the sea to get much rain.

Many parts of the Sahara Desert have steep rocky outcrops like the ones above.

A camel can lose up to 40 per cent of its body weight through dehydration. The fat stored in its hump helps to protect it from the hot Sun.

CAMELS

Camels are superbly adapted to their environment. The hump offers protection from the Sun and also stores fat, which produces energy and water. A camel can store water in its stomach lining and its kidneys can concentrate urine to reduce water loss. It can go for days without water, but when it does find some, can drink 115 litres in ten minutes.

Sometimes mountains prevent winds from dropping moisture and create rain shadow deserts. These include the Mojave and Great Basin deserts of North America and the Patagonian desert. Here wet winds from the sea are forced to rise by mountains. The water vapour in the air cools, condenses and turns to clouds. They rise further, cool and drop their moisture on the windward side of the mountains.

Cool currents along the coast of South Africa have produced the coastal deserts of the Namib and Atacama. The cool winds which blow over these currents cannot hold much moisture.

The effects of desert weather

Hot sunshine during the day heats the desert rocks so they expand. At night the rocks contract or shrink again in the cold. This weathering puts a great strain on the rocks and pieces break off them. The surface splinters into stones and gravel which eventually turn into sand grains.

Windswept sand grains bounce against the rocks, slowly wearing them away. The grains are too heavy for the wind to lift high, so they cut into the rocks near the ground. Some are carved by the wind to look like giant mushrooms. Caves and arches are formed in others.

Desert oases

Oases can be very productive when intensively cultivated. Most African oases were once resting places on caravan routes across the desert. Some depend on springs and wells; others draw waters from rivers entering the desert from nearby mountains with heavy rain or snowfall. There are oases of this kind on the fringes of the Takla-Makan desert at Sinkiang in China, and along the foothills of the Andes mountains.

Green ribbons of cultivated land run along the banks of the Indus, Tigris, Euphrates, Colorado and Rio Grande rivers.

Date palms are grown in the oases of African deserts. Underneath them grow lemons, figs, olives, grapes, apricots, pomegranates, guavas, wheat, maize, millet, beans, peas, onions, tomatoes, sweet potatoes and spices. People prevent drifting sand blowing over their plantations with complex patterns of fences made of palm leaves.

Nomadic peoples

The original people of the deserts were hunter-gatherers or nomads. A few native peoples of the Kalahari, Namib and Australian deserts still hunt and collect wild fruits and seeds. The Bedouin of the deserts of the Middle East and Northern Africa were nomads who lived in tents and bred camels and sheep. The Mongol people of the Gobi desert were also constantly on the move following their herds

Some desert-dwellers escape the heat of the Sun by living in caves, like these in Tunisia.

Date palms in an oasis provide shade and shelter for other crops, such as pomegranates, lemons and apricots.

LONGEST RIVER

The River Nile, the world's longest river, begins in the forested mountains of Burundi. It flows north to the Mediterranean via its delta in north-eastern Egypt. The Nile drains 2,850,000 sq km of land, and its waters support 98 per cent of Egypt's agriculture. The Nile Valley is the world's largest oasis.

of sheep, cattle, goats and camels on horseback. The way of life of many desert peoples has changed. One reason is that governments have made it harder for people to travel between countries. Also, severe droughts have made it more difficult for people and their livestock to survive in the desert, and they can earn more money living in a town or working in a desert oil field or a mine.

Desertification

The world's deserts are growing. This process is called desertification when it is permanent. It is usually the result of a growing number of people and domestic animals living there, eating the grass and cutting down trees for fuel. Without vegetation the soil is washed away by rain or blown away by the wind, Where there are too many people and not enough water, land almost always becomes a desert. This has happened over the last 36 years in the Sahel region, south of the Sahara, and around the Thar desert in India.

Wind-blown sand can engulf palm trees like these growing in a desert oasis.

Spreading oases

Where there is water, the desert can be very fertile. The Sun shines every day, so plants grow quickly. Several crops can be harvested every year. One way of halting the spread of desert is to extend the oases using irrigation so that they provide more food. Since the High Dam was built in Aswan in Egypt, the cultivated area beside the River Nile has grown. Water passing through the sluices of the dam is used for irrigation and also generates hydro-electricity.

Some of the richest farmland in the United States is in southern California. Huge crops of fruit and vegetables are grown all the year round in what was dry desert. Now water from the Colorado River irrigates the land. Similarly, large areas of the Negev Desert in Israel produce crops such as avocados, tomatoes and oranges for export to Europe. But there are drawbacks to building reservoirs and using irrigation. Vast quantities of the water in the reservoir behind the Aswan High Dam evaporates in the Sun. Much of the fertile mud which once spread over the fields when the Nile flooded now clogs the reservoir. The water in many desert areas is slightly salty and when it evaporates from the surface of the soil, it leaves a layer of salt in which plants cannot grow.

Wealth from the desert

The richest desert countries have oil which they sell to pay for imports and development projects. Arabia, Iraq, Iran, Algeria, Libya and Kuwait all have rich oil deposits. Valuable minerals are mined in some desert areas, including gold, silver, diamonds, lead, bauxite, gypsum, uranium, nitrates and phosphates. Tourists also visit many desert areas, attracted by the sunshine and dry, clean air, Today there are probably more people than ever living in deserts, as deep wells, pipelines and tanker lorries can bring them water.

A farmer flooding fields from an irrigation ditch before planting crops in Al-Ula oasis, Saudi Arabia.

The temperate zone

The area between the polar regions and the tropics, north and south of the Equator, is called the temperate zone. The name implies that the temperatures are never extreme, but this is not always true. In fact, the area contains a range of climates and natural landscapes. It also contains some of the world's largest industrialized cities.

Where are the temperate areas?

Most people in the world live in the temperate zone, which includes some of the most fertile places on Earth. In the northern hemisphere it includes northern Europe, including the middle latitudes of European Russia; north-eastern China, Korea and Japan; Washington State, the north-central and north-eastern parts of the United States; the coast of British Columbia and eastern Canada. In the southern hemisphere the temperate zone includes the southern coast of Chile; the south-eastern tip of Australia, Tasmania; and the South Island of New Zealand.

Temperate climates

Places in the temperate zone have four to eight months each year when the mean temperature is above 10°C. Some have severe winters and very hot summers. All areas in the temperate zone have four seasons: spring, summer, autumn and winter. They have oceanic or continental climates. An oceanic climate is milder than a continental one, with year-round mean temperatures of 0°C or above. The western or windward sides of the middle latitudes of continents have this climate.

These cows belong to a dairy farm on the rich pastures of the South Island of New Zealand.

The Dingle Peninsula in County Kerry, Ireland has a mild, unsettled climate because of the Atlantic Ocean.

Places with an oceanic climate have unsettled, cloudy, wet and windy weather for part of the year. The Sun is often out for only 30 to 40 per cent of the total possible time.

Changeable weather

Oceanic climate areas often have unreliable weather. They lie at the ever-changing boundary between warm tropical air blowing towards the poles and cold polar air blowing from the poles. First one air mass, then the other, invades the places which are near the polar fronts of the two hemispheres.

The warming air masses sometimes produce complex low pressure systems called depressions – some several hundred kilometres across. They are most active in autumn or early winter when the temperature difference between land and sea is greatest. Most depressions move east, sometimes at the rate of several hundred kilometres a day, bringing rapid changes of weather. Precipitation in oceanic zones varies with altitude, but is highest when there are most depressions. The west coast of Great Britain has about 1,000 mm of rain a year, which increases to more than 3,000 mm in mountainous areas, such as the Lake District in north-western England or Snowdonia in Wales. East of the mountainous areas, in the rain shadow, rainfall is much less.

Continental climates

Temperate continental climate areas are some of the Earth's most densely populated and economically developed areas. They include the American mid-east and eastern Europe. Here temperature is more seasonal than in oceanic climates, with very cold winters and hot summers. This climate only occurs in the northern hemisphere because there are no large land masses in the southern hemisphere at these latitudes. Continental climates become more severe as you go from south to north and from the east coast inland, especially in the winter. Long, hot summers and a frost-free period of 150 to 200 days a year makes continental climate areas productive for crop farming.

Green lands

Where there is enough moisture, the natural vegetation of the temperate zone is forest: coniferous in the north, giving way further south to deciduous forest. There are extensive areas of grassland in the interior of the continents, where there is too little rainfall for trees. Coniferous forests also grow in the drier, warmer temperate regions around the Mediterranean Sea described in Chapter 11.

FERTILE GROUND

Both modern industry and agriculture first developed in the temperate zone of north-western Europe. As farmers became more efficient they were able to produce surplus food. This helped to make the Industrial Revolution possible, because people did not have to spend all their time trying to grow enough food to eat.

Northern coniferous forests

The largest single area of the northern temperate zone is the evergreen coniferous forest. This is the taiga biome, also called the boreal forest. Spruce, pines, larches, hemlocks and firs grow here. During the winter the water in the soil freezes as temperatures can fall to below -40°C. The tough, needle-shaped leaves of the conifers help to reduce water loss by evaporation when the ground is frozen or during a drought. This huge belt of conifers stretching across the northern hemisphere is 2,000 km wide in places. The forest occupies parts of Scandinavia, northern Europe, Siberia and the width of North America.

These steep slopes by the Black Sea in the Republic of Georgia are covered in dense coniferous forest.

Flora and fauna

In these forests, densely packed trees grow tall and straight. Little light reaches the ground, so few other plants can grow beneath the trees. Most of the trees are evergreens, and shed leaves all the year round rather than during the autumn. Temperatures are low, so the leaves decay slowly, and a deep layer of partly-rotted leaves builds up on the forest floor. These easily catch fire and forest fires are common. The leaf litter produces acids as it decays, which are washed into the soil, carrying iron compounds. These compounds form a layer called a hardpan, which makes the soils unsuitable for most other plants.

Many animals live in the northern coniferous forest. The trees provide food for moose, squirrels, beavers, hares, voles and lemmings, and birds such as the capercaillie, grouse, nutcracker and crossbill. In summer, large numbers of birds migrate there to nest and rear their young on the insects that feed on the conifers. Many carnivores, including lynx, wolves, wolverines and martens, feed on the birds.

People and the forests

Few people live in the northern coniferous forests. Some hunt and trap animals for their fur. Others are lumbermen who fell trees. They may be farm workers from further south, who work in the forests when there is no work on the farms. Logs are floated down rivers to sawmills, or moved by lorry or train. The large logs are cut into planks, and smaller ones are pulped to make paper or card. Much building timber comes from these forests.

Canadian coniferous forests

Coniferous forests cover almost 40 per cent of Canada. It is the world's largest exporter of wood pulp and paper. One in every 12 jobs in Canada depends on wood and the government owns nearly all the forests.

Minerals and mining

Valuable minerals, including gold, silver, copper, iron, nickel and uranium are mined in the northern forest. Oil and coal are also mined there. Some of the largest towns and villages in the forest area have grown up where these minerals are mined.

The brown bears of the northern coniferous forests sleep in caves during the worst of the winter weather.

Conifers provide winter food for the capercaillie and other coniferous forest birds.

ACID RAIN

Large areas of coniferous forest in central Europe, Norway, Sweden and eastern North America are dying because of acid rain. This is caused when factories, power stations and vehicles burn fossil fuels and release poisonous gases into the atmosphere. These gases dissolve in rainwater (or mist, fog, sleet or snow) and form an acid precipitation which can fall huge distances away from where it was formed. This invisible poison destroys trees, kills fish in lakes and rivers, and attacks stone buildings

A lumberman at work high up a pine tree in the coniferous forests of the northern United States.

Temperate grasslands

There are vast areas of grassland in the interiors of the continents in the temperate zone. They grow where there is too little precipitation for trees to grow – usually less than 500 mm a year. Various names are given to these grasslands, including prairie, steppe and pampas.

Temperate grasslands are usually far from the warming effects of the oceans and rain-bearing winds. Summers are hot and dry, and winters may be long and bitterly cold. Winds can fan the flames of accidental fires in late summer and dry the soil. Only on lake shores and along the banks of rivers is there enough moisture to allow trees to grow.

Places and names

The largest area of temperate grasslands in the world is the Eurasian steppes, stretching more than 3,000 km from Hungary through southern Russia to China. The North American prairies stretch from Canada's prairie provinces almost to the Gulf of Mexico, and east to south of the Great Lakes. The pampas are in Argentina, Uruguay and Brazil, stretching from the foothills of the Andes to the Atlantic. The veld in the eastern corner of South Africa is close to the sea and does not suffer the same extremes of temperature. Australia's temperate grasslands occupy most of the basin of the Murray-Darling River.

Bison (buffalo) once roamed the North American prairies in their millions, but were brought close to extinction by early settlers. They now live in protected herds.

The prairies

Great herds of pronghorn antelopes and bison (buffalo) used to feed on the North American prairies. In the 19th century, white people began to settle there and created sheep and cattle ranches. They killed most of the bison, first for food, later to be rid of them. Eventually the settlers began to cultivate the prairies.

Today most of the land is planted with wheat, oats, barley and maize. Canada is one of the world's largest wheat producers. Prairie farms are very large and widely spaced. The ploughing, sowing and harvesting are all done by groups of machines. The growing season is short, so farmers plant varieties of wheat that ripen quickly. Harvesting begins in August in the southern prairies, later further north. Lorries take the ripe grain to storage towers (elevators) built beside railways. Later the grain is taken by rail to ports from where ships take it all over the world.

A team of combine harvesters works on the wheat harvest in Washington State, United States.

The Dust Bowl

Where soil is dry and unprotected by plants it easily blows away. The finest soil particles blow away first, leaving the less fertile larger ones. During the 1920s large areas of grassland in the Great Plains of the United States were ploughed and planted with cereal crops. The same crops were grown year after year, and the overworked soil became dry and powdery. During the early 1930s, there was a severe drought, and in 1934 a gale swept across the United States, picking up 350,000 tonnes of dust. Birds suffocated in mid-air and cities were plunged into darkness as dust clouds blotted out the Sun. More than 350,000 people abandoned their homes and farmers were ruined. Thousands died of starvation, or lung diseases caused by breathing in the dusty air. Russia had similar dustbowl erosion after the Second World War.

Surplus wheat piled up by a grain storage tower, or elevator, in Kansas in the United States.

Vanishing grasslands and animals

Many kinds of natural grassland are becoming rare. About two-thirds of the Canadian prairies and half the United States prairies have been converted into huge cereal farms. There is little natural vegetation left. Much of the South African veld has also been destroyed. Some is used for grazing sheep, and maize is grown on higher land. There are a few springbok antelopes left in game reserves and national parks. The bison and wild horses which once grazed the steppes have gone, and the wolves which preyed on them are now rare.

Temperate deciduous forests

There are two main tree types in forests: broad-leaved and coniferous. The latter usually have needle-shaped leaves and most are evergreen, losing leaves through the year rather than during the autumn. In temperate climates deciduous trees shed all their leaves during the winter.

STORM FELLED

Fifteen million trees, mostly deciduous, blew down in one night when hurricane-force winds hit Britain in October 1987.

Coniferous and deciduous forests

Coniferous forest occupies the largest single area of the northern temperate zone, where soils are poor and winters very cold. Further south are the broad-leaved trees of the temperate deciduous forests. These occupy the eastern half of North America from southern Ontario and Quebec to northern Florida, most of Europe (outside Scandinavia, high mountains and the Mediterranean), eastern China and Japan. In the southern hemisphere there are similar deciduous forests in parts of southern Australia, New Zealand, South Africa and South America.

SUN CATCHER

A small oak tree with a trunk 60 cm in diameter has about 100,000 leaves, with a total area of about 500m² (roughly equivalent to two tennis courts). This adaptation helps the tree catch the maximum amount of sunlight in summer.

Broad-leaved beech woodland in the forests of Bavaria, Germany. These forests grow in deep, fertile soils.

The main trees in temperate deciduous woodlands are oak, ash, elm, beech, chestnut and maple. Most of the precipitation falls as rain, evenly distributed through the year. Winters are short, but cold enough to slow growth and photosynthesis as the trees shed their leaves.

Seasons in a deciduous forest

In a deciduous forest there are big differences between the seasons. During the winter the trees are bare, and a thick carpet of fallen leaves covers the forest floor. Only a few animals are active. Hedgehogs, dormice, chipmunks and black bears hibernate.

In spring temperatures rise and the fallen leaves rapidly decompose. Slugs, snails, woodlice, millipedes and earthworms feed on them, breaking them into smaller pieces in their droppings. Bacteria and fungi in the soil then turn the leaves into a deep, rich, fertile layer of humus. Smaller plants on the forest floor, such as bluebells, primroses and violets, grow fast, flower and produce seeds before the trees above open their leaves. Oak and beech trees produce green flowers, fertilised by pollen carried on the wind. Maple, lime and chestnut trees have bright or fragrant flowers which attract pollen-carrying insects.

Deciduous tree branches spread widely to catch the summer sunshine. As the leaves open, insects hatch on the branches to feed on them. Thousands of insect-eating birds arrive from further south. Their nesting and breeding is timed so they can feed their young on the multitudes of insects and their larvae. Deer also feed on the tree leaves.

During spring small plants on the deciduous forest floor, such as these bluebells, grow rapidly and flower. They produce seeds before the tree leaves above have opened.

During the autumn nuts, acorns, beechmast and chestnuts provide food for a variety of animals. Jays, squirrels and wood mice store the tree fruits and seeds. The days become shorter and colder. The trees can no longer take enough water from the soil and their leaves die and turn yellow, orange, red or brown before they fall. Fruiting bodies of mushrooms and toadstools appear above the soil or on tree trunks. The spores of the fungi feed many tiny animals in the soil.

How a forest evolves

Deciduous forest is the natural climax vegetation of warmer parts of the temperate zone. If bare ground is left untouched, this type of forest returns. In 1882 a wheat field in England was fenced and left alone. Wild grasses quickly covered the field. These were replaced by taller weeds and then by shrubs and small trees. Now the field is covered by oak woodland identical to older woodland in the area. Each stage in this succession offers different habitats and foods for animals, and as each stage is passed any animals that are unable to adapt die.

Deciduous trees in their autumn colours in Minnesota in the United States.

Using trees

In Stone Age times people used wood for arrows, clubs and tool handles, as well as fuel. Today wood is still an important fuel in many parts of the world. It is also used for buildings, fences, bridges and furniture. Many musical instruments, toys and tools have wood in them. Some wood comes from natural forests, but most now comes from plantations – man-made forests planted and managed by people.

Cork, charcoal, turpentine and some paper and artificial silk or rayon also come from the trees that grow in temperate forests. Apples, pears, plums, chestnuts, hazelnuts and walnuts are all harvested from deciduous trees in temperate areas.

A kiln producing charcoal from unwanted wood. Charcoal is still an important fuel used in the chemical industry as well as by artists.

THIRSTY TREES

Every tree needs an enormous amount of water every day. Water passes from the roots up the trunk and evaporates from the leaves. As much as 900 litres pass up and out of an average oak tree every day.

Disappearing forests

Temperate deciduous forests originally covered much of Europe and the eastern half of North America, parts of Japan and eastern and north-central Asia, as well as parts of southern Chile and Argentina in South America. These areas include some of the most densely-populated and heavily-industrialized parts of the world.

For 10,000 years forests have been cleared to make way for farmland, towns and cities, and to provide timber and firewood. Most of the deciduous forest in China disappeared so long ago that scientists do not know what trees it contained. Magnificent forests of oak, chestnut, hornbeam and pine grew around the Mediterranean as recently as 2,000 years ago. In Europe and North America there are still large areas of deciduous woodland. This is mostly secondary forest, which developed by succession after the original forest was cleared, or managed forest, planted and selectively cut at intervals, sometimes to encourage birds and mammals that can be hunted. Some evidence of the original primary forests exists, but mostly it has vanished.

Coppiced deciduous woodland, an example of a managed forest in Cambridgeshire.

Disappearing animals

As the deciduous forests have disappeared, so too have many of the large animals that once lived there. Large carnivores, such as the wolf and lynx, have been driven into coniferous forests. Wild boar now live mainly in game reserves, while red deer have taken to moorland. When red deer move back into deciduous forests they quickly become destructive pests, as there are no longer any large carnivores to keep down their numbers. Smaller animals, such as foxes, stoats and weasels, have learned to live in the wooded fringes of fields. Foxes have also adapted to living in towns and cities, scavenging rather than hunting for food.

Farmland and crops

In Europe, most of the natural forest has been cleared for agriculture or replaced by man-made forests and plantations. Much of the land is arable, growing crops such as cereals, potatoes, sugar beet and oil seed rape. Grassland is mainly artificial, with just one or two species of grass that are regularly fertilized and treated with weedkiller. If the land is protected from grazing, such grasslands may revert to scrubland and then to secondary woodland, but this does not contain the huge diversity of plant and animal species that inhabited the original deciduous woodland.

Red deer are controlled by shooting in many deciduous forests because they no longer have natural predators.

Fertile soils

In moist temperate regions, the soils that developed under deciduous woodland are generally easy to farm intensively. There are many hours of sunshine during the growing season, evenly distributed rainfall and few droughts. So a wide variety of crops can be grown in the deep, fertile soils and harvested at different times. Some farmers use a rotation system to give high yields. Today, they more often use chemical pesticides and fertilizers for this purpose.

A crop of oil-seed rape growing on fertile soil that once supported deciduous forest in Norfolk, England.

Mediterranean climates

Mediterranean climates are warm temperate climates.
named after the regions bordering the Mediterranean Sea.
Other parts of the world with a similar climate are parts
of South Africa, Australia, Chile and California in the US.

*Umbrella pines growing near the
Mediterranean in southern Spain.*

CORK TREES

*Cork is used to close
wine bottles, for mats,
floats, as a sound
absorber and as
insulation. The outer
bark is stripped from
cork oaks every nine
years, during July and
August. The increasing
use of plastic corks
for wine bottles is
endangering these trees.*

There are Mediterranean climates between
latitudes 30 and 40° north and south of the
Equator, mainly on the western side of
continents. During the summer, warm dry
winds blow from the Equator, bringing dry
conditions. In the winter the winds swing
towards the Equator and westerly winds
bring rain. Summers are hot, and winters
are usually warm enough for plants to grow.

In the area around the Mediterranean,
the sea has a big effect on the climate. In the
summer, it is cooler than the land, so the air
sinks down over the sea and the surrounding
area and there is very little rain. Few clouds
mean high temperatures. In winter the sea
is warmer than the land, so the surrounding
land enjoys mild winters, while the warm,
moist air from the sea brings rain. In other
parts of the world with this climate, cold
ocean currents affect the local climate.

Mediterranean vegetation

Grass does not grow well in these areas.
Magnificent forests of oak, chestnut,
hornbeam and pine grew there around
2,000 years ago. The few trees that survive
now have long roots to reach water deep
underground, or thick bark, like the cork oak
tree. Some have small waxy leaves or needle-
like leaves to avoid moisture loss. Evergreen
scrub is now the most typical vegetation.

Farming and crops

The main cereal of the Mediterranean lands is
wheat. Areas with this climate are important
wine producers. The grape vine, with its long
roots and tough bark, is well adapted to the
climate. Olives have been a staple food for
centuries, supplying oil in a region where milk
and butter are hard to produce. Figs, peaches,

The climate in Andalucia in Spain is perfect for growing olives. These olive groves provide a good supply of olive oil every year.

almonds, apricots, cherries, oranges, lemons, grapefruit and limes are grown. In many countries farmers plant crops under plastic polytunnels, and irrigate them to grow vegetables all year round. Israel has become almost self-sufficient in food in spite of the fact that much of its land is desert, by irrigating with water from underground or the mountains.

Arid areas can be made productive by using machinery for irrigation, to spread fertilisers and pesticides, for frost control, picking, packing and distribution. The development of irrigation and transport transformed the Great Valley of California. The valley stretches 750 km north to south and has a surplus of water in the north and a shortage in the south. One of the world's greatest engineering schemes collects water from the Sacramento River in the north and carries it south to a pumping station. This raises the water to a canal that carries it further south, where the water is used to maintain the level of the San Joaquin River, and irrigate the dry southern part of the Great Valley.

Tourism

Tourism has become a major industry for many areas bordering the Mediterranean Sea. The hot, dry summers in Greece, Spain, Italy and southern France, and Morocco and Tunisia in North Africa, have made them popular holiday destinations for northern Europeans. Resorts of hotels and holiday villas and apartments, together with restaurants, bars and nightclubs have developed in strips along the coast.

Tourism is a major industry along the shores of the Mediterranean. This crowded beach is in Cannes in southern France.

Village life

Away from the coast village life often continues as it has done for centuries. Farmers intensively cultivate fruit and vegetables close to their villages, where they can give their crops frequent attention and control irrigation. Away from the villages, farmers grow cereal crops on the better soils. Sheep and goats browse beneath the olive groves, and can overgraze the dry hillsides.

Polar regions

12

The polar regions are cold, icy deserts. During the winter the Antarctic regions around the South Pole are the coldest places on Earth. It is bitterly cold even at the height of summer. The northern Arctic region is less cold but still icy all year round. Very few people live here, and those who do have to cope with the constant cold.

The Antarctic continent is almost completely covered by ice and snow. It is surrounded by a deep ocean, partly covered with floating ice.

COLDEST CONTINENT

Antarctica is the highest, coldest, windiest continent on Earth. It is bigger than India and China combined, and 98 per cent is covered by a sheet of ice with an average thickness of 2,000m. About 90 per cent of the world's ice and 7 per cent of its fresh water is in Antarctica.

The Antarctic and Arctic regions

The Antarctic region around the South Pole includes a huge continent almost covered with ice and snow. A deep ocean partly covered with floating ice even in summer, surrounds it. By contrast, the northern polar region is an ocean basin surrounded by land. Floating ice covers much of the Arctic Ocean all year round. The ice is so thick that even the strongest surface ships cannot reach the North Pole. There is no day and night in either region, instead there are five or six months of darkness in winter, followed by five or six months of summer daylight. There is no east or west; at the South Pole every direction is north, and at the North Pole every direction is south.

Why are the polar regions so cold?

The polar regions are so very cold because the Sun's rays never shine straight down on them. This means that, even in summer, the Sun never seems to climb high in the sky. Although the Sun may shine all day and all night, it gives very little warmth to the ground or air. Because there is so much white snow and ice, many of the Sun's rays are reflected back into space and never reach the ground to warm it. In winter there is no warming effect from the Sun because it never rises above the horizon. For these reasons the polar regions never warm up.

At the South Pole the mean air temperature for January, the warmest month, is -28.6°C. For the coldest month (July) it is -59.7°C. Constant strong winds make the cold seem even more severe. The North Pole is warmer, with summer temperatures occasionally above freezing, and mean winter temperatures down to about -30°C. This is because more of it lies close to sea level. The coldest parts of this region lie far from the sea, on the high icy plain of Greenland, and the northerly parts of Canada and Siberia.

Around the North Pole

The North Pole is on a huge floating ice floe, which is about the size of a football field, with ice two or three metres thick. The nearest land is 700 km away on the coast of Greenland. Ice floes cover the Arctic Ocean all year round. In warmer parts of the Arctic lands, ice and snow disappear in summer, and tundra plants grow on the stony ground. The tundra is the biome with the coldest climate. It has 10-40 cm of precipitation (mainly snow) every year. There are no trees, only knee-high grasses and shrubs. The topsoil thaws in summer, but half a metre down is the permafrost, where the ground is always frozen. In winter the soil freezes solid, and lakes and rivers have a thick covering of ice. The few animals that survive here include polar bears, musk oxen, reindeer, caribou, Arctic foxes, Arctic hares and lemmings. Along its southern edge the tundra merges into the great northern coniferous forests along the tree-line.

Around the South Pole

The South Pole is high on an ice cap, with 3,000m of solid ice beneath. A plain of ice and snow surrounds it, carved by the wind into ripples and furrows. In summer the Sun shines, but the air is bitingly cold. In winter it is dark and much colder, Not far away lies a US scientific research station called Amundsen-Scott, in honour of the first two men who led expeditions to the South Pole. The Antarctic ice cap is formed from snow that over thousands of years has turned into ice under its own weight. It has slowly moved downhill to fill the valleys and cover the plains of the continent beneath. In places the ice is more than 4 km thick and there are mountain ranges underneath, bigger than the European Alps.

This is a lichen known as reindeer moss. Lichens are typical plants of the Arctic tundra.

Living in the Arctic

Warmly dressed people can work outside at temperatures of -30 to -40°C, if the air is still. Winds make everything feel colder. At -45°C breath steams and freezes. Intense cold can cause frostbite on hands, feet and faces and reflected sunlight can cause snow blindness. The Arctic climate is harsh, but many different peoples from central Asia, Europe and North America live there. In the past, they didn't develop settled civilizations because they couldn't grow crops. Until recently they travelled for a living, hunting, fishing, herding caribou or reindeer, and trading with neighbouring groups.

The Inuit people

Until 40 or 50 years ago the Inuit lived in the Arctic, hunting whales and fishing. They ate the flesh of these animals cooked, dried or raw. In winter seal was the main food. Seals also provided clothing, materials for tents, boats and harpoon lines, and fuel for light and heat. In the summer, the Inuit lived in sealskin tents. Winter houses were stone-built and covered with moss or turf. During long journeys the Inuit built temporary winter homes, or igloos, of snow blocks. Today their old skills are dying out. They hunt with rifles and harpoons, and many travel by snowmobile rather than a dog team. Most Inuit now live in permanent homes and many have learned trades. The main reason for this change is that the Arctic is rich in oil, gas, copper, uranium and other valuable minerals. Oil and gas are important in North America. In Alaska oil is produced at Prudhoe Bay, heated and piped across the mountains and valleys southwards to the giant Valdez oil terminal. From here it is taken by ship to the west coast ports of the US. The pipeline carries 17 per cent of US domestic oil.

Modern Inuit hunters use a rifle, although some occasionally still travel by dog sledge.

Wooden houses on stilts in an Inuit village in the Thule district of Greenland.

New roads, railways and cities

A road, called the Alaska Highway, has been built from the United States through Canada to Alaska. New railways and industrial cities are being built where there was once tundra or forest. In Siberia, coal, iron ore, diamonds, gold, oil and natural gas are extracted and refined. New towns and power stations have been built. The problem with constructing buildings and oil pipelines on the tundra is that if the buildings melt the permafrost under them they will sink. To prevent this happening, buildings and pipelines are raised on pilings.

Life in Antarctica

Antarctica has such a harsh climate that people have never settled there permanently. Its only inhabitants are visiting scientists who carry out research projects. There are more than 40 research stations operating all the year round and many more summer-only stations. They belong to 18 different countries. Scientists study the unique wildlife, the weather and climate, the ice and glaciers, rocks, volcanoes and earthquakes, and the upper atmosphere. Research stations are usually a couple of well-insulated huts with radio masts and fuel tanks outside. Generators provide electricity. The largest stations are on the coast, so that in summer ships can bring fresh supplies. Inland stations are smaller, as they have to be built and supplied by aircraft or tractor-train.

ICEBERGS

Icebergs are huge chunks of freshwater ice. The world's tallest iceberg was discovered off the coast of Greenland in 1958. It was 168m above the water. The world's largest iceberg broke away from the Ross Ice Shelf in Antarctica in 2000. It was 295 km long and 37 km wide, with a surface area about the size of the Gambia.

Polar tourism

The Arctic and Antarctic are growing in popularity. Tourists visit them to see the beautiful wilderness areas and wildlife in its natural surroundings. But the fuels they use to get there, the waste they leave behind, and the disturbance they cause to the wildlife and the native people (in the Arctic) can all cause problems. In the future it may become necessary to control the numbers of tourists visiting.

Tourists come ashore from a cruise liner to observe a penguin colony in Antarctica.

Mountain climates

High mountains and mountain ranges cover about
5 per cent of the Earth's land surface. Mountain ranges
have more than one type of climate, partly because the
higher up a mountain you go the colder it becomes. The
air also becomes thinner so that it can store less heat.

Mountain weather and vegetation

Mountains force moisture-laden clouds to rise, cool and deposit water
as rain or snow. Temperature falls with altitude, at about 2°C for every
300m. The tops of the highest mountains are always snow-capped.
The snow-line is at 5,000-5,500m near the Equator, 2,700m in the
European Alps, and at sea level near the poles. After dark, the thin air
loses heat rapidly and the temperatures plummet.

The reduction in temperature and stronger winds result in
vegetation zones on a mountain. In the European Alps, deciduous trees
grow only in valleys and on the lower slopes. Above are coniferous
forests that give way at the tree-line to pasture and a tundra zone
before permanent snow cover. Vegetation zones can differ from one
side of a mountain to the other. Slopes facing the Sun may have
different climates from those facing away from it. Leeward slopes
(facing away from the wind) have much less rain than windward ones.

*Mountains in the
Bavarian alps,
Germany clearly
show the tree-line
and snow-line.*

HIGHEST RANGE

*The world's highest
mountain range is
the Himalayas, on
the northern border
of the Indian sub-
continent. The
Himalayas contain
all 14 of the world's
peaks higher than
8,000m, including
the world's highest,
Mount Everest
(8,850m). The
Himalayas are
a young mountain
range and
still growing.*

Flowering plants above the tree-line on mountains are very similar to those in the Arctic tundra.

Mountain winds

Winds may become warmer as they cross mountains. As moist air rises over mountains it cools slowly and rain falls. The air is drier and may warm faster as it descends on the leeward side. The Chinook blows from the Rocky Mountains to the Canadian prairies, raising the temperature by 10 or 20°C in a few minutes. It melts the snow, so that spring wheat can be sown. Winds forced through valleys strengthen. In the South of France, a wind called the Mistral is funnelled by the Rhone valley and brings cold, blustery weather from the north.

People and mountains

Valley bottoms and low mountain slopes facing the Sun are often farmed. In the European Alps and Norway, cattle and goats are kept indoors in winter and driven up to high pastures in spring. Traditionally their milk is made into cheese. Small petrol-driven cultivators and grass cutters have replaced hand tools and motor transport means that herdsmen no longer need to live in the high mountains in summer.

Many people visit mountains to walk, rock-climb, pot-hole, hang-glide, snowboard or ski. In parts of India and Africa, people go to the mountains because they are cooler in the summer, although breathing can be difficult at higher altitudes because there is less oxygen in the air.

Mountains in the future

Mountain regions, like other areas of the world, can tell us a great deal about what happened in the past, for example, during the Ice Ages. They are also vulnerable to the effects of climate change, such as acid rain and global warming, which are described in detail in *Changing Climates*, another book in this series.

Cattle spend the summer on the high pastures in the Swiss Alps. During the winter they are kept indoors in the valleys and fed on hay or silage prepared the previous summer.

Glossary

air pressure The force of the air pressing down on the Earth's surface.

atmosphere The blanket of gases around a planet, held there by the pull of the planet's gravity.

biome A large zone of plants and animals that are adapted to a particular type of climate and soil.

canyon A deep gorge, often with a stream or river.

climate The average weather in a place over a long period of time.

climax vegetation The final stage in the development of the natural vegetation of a region. This is normally determined by the climate and soil.

continental climate The climate of the interior of a continent, which has great extremes of temperature between summer and winter.

Coriolis effect The way that the direction of winds is turned by the spin of the Earth – to the right in the northern hemisphere and to the left in the southern hemisphere. The Coriolis force is strongest at the poles and weakens towards the Equator, where it disappears altogether.

current A body of air or water moving in a definite direction.

deciduous A tree or shrub which sheds all its leaves at a certain season every year.

desert A dry region of the world in which few plants are able to grow.

desertification The process of making or becoming a desert, usually as a result of human activity.

drought A long period of dry weather, with no rainfall.

dune A hill or ridge of loose sand which has been blown into drifts by the wind.

ecosystem A system formed by the interaction of all living things and the soil and climate of the area in which they live.

Equator The imaginary line around the centre of the Earth.

erosion The gradual wearing away of the Earth's surface.

evergreen A tree which does not lose all its leaves in autumn or the dry season, but loses them a few at a time throughout the year.

fossil fuel A fuel produced from the fossil remains of plants or animals: coal, peat, oil or natural gas.

global warming The warming of the Earth's atmosphere due to air pollution.

greenhouse effect The warming of the Earth caused by certain gases in the atmosphere, called greenhouse gases. These allow the Sun's rays to reach the Earth's surface, but trap heat given off by the ground.

ice cap A permanent covering of ice over a highland area or island.

ice floe Any separate large piece of floating sea ice.

irrigation Watering the land by artificial means so that crops will grow.

latitude The distance of any point on the Earth's surface, north or south of the Equator, measured in degrees.

maritime climate A climate directly affected by the nearness of the sea. It occurs mainly on islands and has relatively mild winters and cool summers. It is very similar to an oceanic climate.

microclimate The climate of a very small area.

monsoon A wind which blows from different directions at different times of the year, causing wet and dry seasons, particularly in southern Asia, northern Australia and western Africa.

nomad Someone who has no permanent home, but moves from place to place in search of food or pasture.

oasis A place in a desert where there is fresh water, allowing settlements and agriculture to be established.

oceanic climate A climate that is mild because of the moderating effects of the surrounding water.

permafrost Ground which is permanently frozen.

photosynthesis The process by which green plants make their food using simple raw materials and sunlight energy.

plantation A forest which has been planted by people to produce crops that are then sold.

plateau An area of high, level land.

precipitation Any form of water (solid or liquid) that falls from the atmosphere and reaches the ground.

rain shadow An area of decreased rainfall on the lee, or sheltered, side of a hill or mountain.

rotation A farming system in which a succession of different crops is grown on the same piece of land to maintain the fertility of the soil.

savanna The natural open tropical grassland with scattered trees and shrubs covering vast areas of Africa, South America and northern Australia.

shifting cultivation A type of farming in which people clear a piece of land and grow crops on it for a few years until the soil is no longer fertile. The people then move on to farm a new area of land.

snow-line The lowest level on a mountain above which snow never completely disappears.

spring A flow of water from the ground. Many streams and rivers have a spring as their source.

succession The gradual development of natural vegetation to the climax vegetation.

subsistence farming Farming in which most or all of what is grown is eaten or used by the farmer and his family, with little or nothing left over to sell.

taiga Cold, coniferous forest in the northern hemisphere.

temperate climate A moderate climate without extremes of temperature.

trade winds Steady winds in the tropics blowing from the north-east in the northern hemisphere and from the south-east in the southern hemisphere.

tree-line The upper limit of tree growth on a mountain.

tropics The hot regions of the Earth on either side of the Equator where the Sun is directly overhead at midday.

tropical rainforest The natural vegetation covering the wooded parts of the tropics.

troposphere The layer of the atmosphere that lies closest to the Earth, where our weather occurs.

tundra The treeless lands around the Arctic Ocean.

water vapour Water in the form of an invisible gas.

weather What is happening in the atmosphere at any particular time and place in terms of clouds, humidity, sunshine, temperature, visibility, precipitation, air pressure and wind.

weathering The action of the weather in breaking down rocks on the Earth's surface.

xerophyte A plant adapted to very dry conditions, for example, in a desert.

Index